Usborne Beginners

Night animals

Susan Meredith
Designed by Nicola Butler
and Josephine Thompson

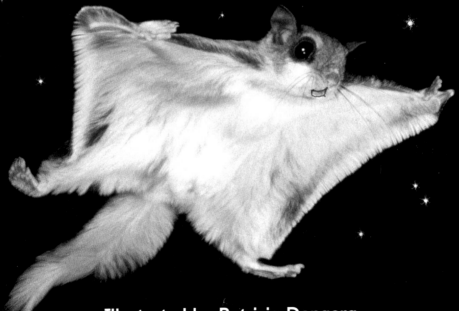

Illustrated by Patrizia Donaera
and Adam Larkum

Night animals consultant: Margaret Rostron

Reading consultant: Alison Kelly
Roehampton University of Surrey

This is a photo of a flying squirrel. The cover photo shows a dormouse.

Contents

Busy at night

Thousands of animals are out
and about at night. They are
called nocturnal animals.

Raccoons are nocturnal.
They stay wide-awake all night.

3

Night feasts

Night animals eat in the dark. Some find more food at night. Others feel safer then.

A leopard waits for an animal to pass by.

It leaps down and kills it with a bite.

It drags it up into a tree to eat it.

Night monkeys eat fruit. They grab their share while other monkeys are asleep.

Big birds can attack koalas. Koalas munch leaves at night, while the birds are asleep.

Bushbabies

Bushbabies are night animals that live in trees.

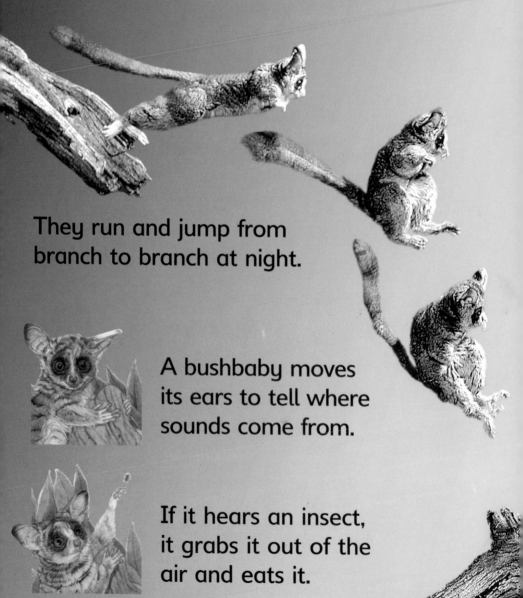

They run and jump from
branch to branch at night.

A bushbaby moves
its ears to tell where
sounds come from.

If it hears an insect,
it grabs it out of the
air and eats it.

A mother bushbaby carries her baby around in her mouth.

She leaves it clinging to a twig while she goes to look for food.

A bushbaby's long tail helps it balance in the air.

Bushbabies comb their fur with one long claw.

Big eyes

Lots of night animals have big bulgy eyes.
This helps them to see in the dark.

Tarsiers have
the biggest eyes
of any animal
their size.

This tarsier has caught a
huge insect to eat but it
can spot tiny ones too.

8

Geckos open their eyes wide to see in the dark.

Light hurts a night animal's eyes. The black part shrinks in the day to keep light out.

Some frogs' eyes narrow to a thin slit in daylight.

The black part of a tiger's eyes shrinks to a dot.

Geckos peer out from four tiny holes in a slit.

Listen and sniff

It isn't always easy to see in the dark. Night animals need to smell and hear well too.

Aardvarks have long ears and long snouts.

They listen for ants and sniff out their nests.

Aardvarks dig up ants' nests with their claws.

They trap the ants on their sticky tongue.

Gila monsters sniff and lick the ground to tell if there is food around.

Fennec foxes are the smallest foxes in the world but they have the biggest ears.

They can hear mice, lizards and even insects from a long way off.

Owls

Owls are lucky birds. They find lots to eat but nothing wants to eat them.

An owl has big wings. It doesn't need to flap them a lot.

Its feathers are soft and fluffy. They don't make a noise.

Other animals don't hear the owl coming and get pounced on.

Owls can't move their eyes but can turn their heads all the way around to see behind them.

Owls can see and hear very well. This owl's ears are not where you might expect.

Feathers

Ear

Too hot

Some animals can't stand the heat of the sun and come out at night when it is cooler.

At night, hippos feed on grass.

In the day they sit in water to cool off. They cover themselves with mud like a sunblock.

Slugs come out at night because they would dry up and die in the sun.

Kangaroo rats live in hot deserts. They dig burrows under the sand with their feet. It is cooler underground.

At night the rats hop around like kangaroos.

They pick up seeds and stuff them in their mouths.

They empty them in their burrows to eat next day.

Daytime sleep

Most night animals stay in their home during the day and go to sleep.

Dormice make nests of hay to sleep in.

Nut to eat

Badgers live underground.

They carry their bedding under their chin and sometimes bring it up to air in the sun.

16

Sloths spend their lives
hanging upside down in trees.
They even sleep this way.

Sloths move around
so little that plants
grow in their hair.

17

Keeping hidden

Night animals need to be safe while they rest in the day. Their enemies mustn't see them.

Elephant hawkmoths rest on pink and green plants so they are harder to see.

If opossums are in danger, they pretend to be dead, so enemies leave them alone.

Red-eyed tree frogs hide on leaves in the daytime, like this.

If they get woken up, their bright eyes and legs scare off enemies.

This bird is a frogmouth. The marks on its feathers make it look like a branch.

Bats

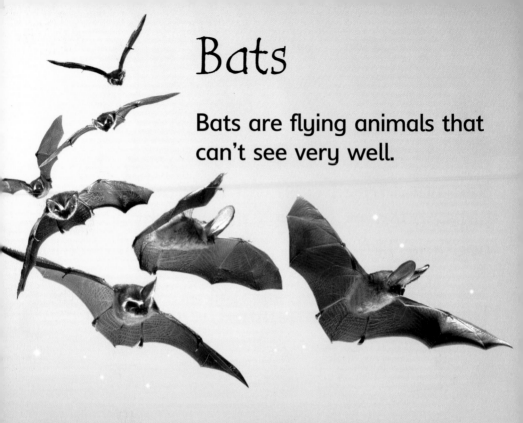

Bats are flying animals that can't see very well.

Some bats eat insects. They find them by using their ears in a strange way.

A bat makes lots of high squeaks as it flies along.

The squeaks hit an insect and bounce back off it.

The bat hears the squeaks. It scoops up the insect.

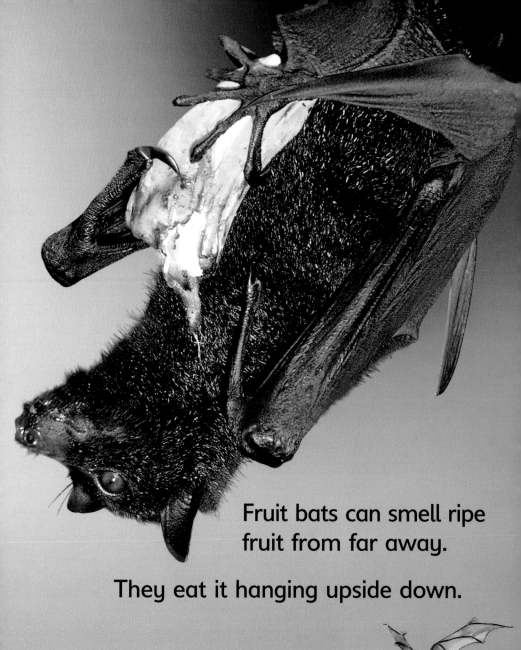

Fruit bats can smell ripe
fruit from far away.

They eat it hanging upside down.

Some bats eat fish, which they grab
out of the water with their claws.

Night noises

While people are fast asleep, animals call to each other in the dark.

Wolves can recognize each other's voices.

They howl to other wolves in their pack, and to tell outsiders to keep away.

Night monkey families don't
like other families to come too close.
They chatter at them until they go away.

A male cricket chirps
a song by rubbing
his wings together.

A female likes the
song and comes to
find the male.

Light messages

Some night animals have strange ways of sending messages.

Fireflies flash like lights to send signals to one another. This tree is full of fireflies.

A firefly makes a flash with its tummy.

Frogs eat fireflies. If they eat too many, they glow.

Black dragonfish have a
light dangling from their
chin. Shrimps come to
look at it and are eaten.

Female glow-worms
can make their bodies
glow with light.

Male glow-worms
fly to meet the
glowing females.

Hedgehogs

Hedgehogs hunt for food at night when there are insects, worms and slugs around.

A hedgehog sniffs out worms, then digs them up.

If a fox comes, the hedgehog rolls itself into a prickly ball.

The fox is hungry but doesn't like prickles, so it goes away.

These baby hedgehogs are only a few days old.

They haven't opened their eyes yet and their prickles are not too sharp.

If a snake attacks a hedgehog, it can be killed on its prickles.

Night and day

Some animals are out and about
in the day as well as at night.

Tigers and other big cats
hunt mainly at night. Smaller
cats like to do the same.

A cat's eyes
shine brightly
in the dark.

Kangaroos are
mostly night
animals although
they sunbathe
in the daytime.

Rabbits get too hot in the day and too cold at night.

They come out just as it is getting dark or getting light.

Foxes used to come out only at night to find other animals to eat.

Now, they come out in the day too, to eat food scraps that people leave lying around.

Glossary

Here are some of the words in this book you might not know. This page tells you what they mean.

 nocturnal - awake and busy at night. Nocturnal animals rest during the day.

 hunt - to look for, catch and kill animals, usually to eat.

 snout - the long nose and mouth parts of an animal's face.

 claw - the hard, sharp, curved parts at the end of animals' fingers or toes.

 burrow - a hole or tunnel that an animal digs in the ground to live in.

 male - an animal that can become a father. Boys and men are male.

 female - an animal that can become a mother. Girls and women are female.

Web sites to visit

If you have a computer, you can find out more about night animals on the Internet. On the Usborne Quicklinks Web site there are links to four fun Web sites.

Web site 1 - Learn about all kinds of night animals and print out pictures of them to shade in.

Web site 2 - See photos of owls and listen to their calls.

Web site 3 - Print out bat pictures to shade in and do a bat jigsaw puzzle.

Web site 4 - Listen to a raccoon.

To visit these Web sites, go to **www.usborne-quicklinks.com** and type the keywords "beginners night animals". Then, click on the link for the Web site you want to visit. Before you use the Internet, look at the safety guidelines inside the back cover of this book and ask an adult to read them with you.

Index

Acknowledgements

Managing editor: Fiona Watt, Managing designer: Mary Cartwright
Photographic manipulation by John Russell, Emma Julings and Zoe Wray

Photo credits

The publishers are grateful to the following for permission to reproduce material: © **Alamy Images** 13,
© **Bruce Coleman** (Alain Compost) 8, (Kim Taylor) 20 and 28; © **CORBIS** (Joe McDonald) 1,
(W. Perry Conway) 3, (George McCarthy) 16, (Staffan Widstrand) 19; © **FLPA – Images of Nature**
(A. Christiansen) 11, (Foto Natura Stock) 17, (Chris Mattison) 18, (Albert Visage) 21, (Mark Newman) 22;
© **Getty Images** (Gary Bell) 5, (JH Pete Carmichael) 9, (Jonathon Gale) 29; © **Heather Angel**
(Peter David) 25; **Nature Picture Library** (David Shale) 25; © **NHPA** (Stephen Dalton) 6-7,
(Christophe Ratier) 14, (Dr Ivan Polunin) 24; © **Oxford Scientific Films** (Owen Newman) cover,
(Alan Root/SAL) 10, (Doug Bertran/SAL) 15; © **Science Photo Library** (Gregory Dimijian) 23;
© **Warren Photographic** (Jane Burton) 27. Photograph on page 31 by Tim Flach.

Internet safety rules

- Ask your parent's or guardian's permission before you connect to the Internet.

- When you are on the Internet, never tell anyone your full name, address or telephone number, and ask an adult before you give your e-mail address.

- If a Web site asks you to log in or register by typing your name or e-mail address, ask an adult's permission first.

- If you do receive an e-mail from someone you don't know, tell an adult and do not reply to the e-mail.

Notes for parents or guardians

The Web sites described in this book are regularly reviewed and the links in Usborne Quicklinks are updated. However, the content of a Web site may change at any time and Usborne Publishing is not responsible, and does not accept liability, for the content or availability of any Web site other than its own, or for any exposure to harmful, offensive or inaccurate material which may appear on the Web. We recommend that children are supervised while on the Internet, that they do not use Internet Chat Rooms and that you use Internet filtering software to block unsuitable material. Please ensure that your children follow the safety guidelines printed above. For more information, see the "Net Help" area on the Usborne Quicklinks Web site at **www.usborne-quicklinks.com**